# HOLY BITES

## HOW TO SPICE UP YOUR DANIEL FAST

# Bringing You Tasty Recipes As You Journey Through Prayer & Fasting

Eugenia George

Photography by Matt George

CaringCarrot.com

Gazpacho, p. 52

To my little darling, Bella Natalia.
You are a testimony of God's unfailing love...


EVERY GOOD GIFT AND EVERY PERFECT GIFT IS
FROM ABOVE, COMING DOWN FROM THE
FATHER OF LIGHTS WITH WHOM THERE IS NO
VARIATION OR SHADOW DUE TO CHANGE.
JAMES 1:17

Daniel Fast Paella p. 26

# TABLE OF CONTENTS:

# INTRODUCTION

I ate no choice food; no meat or wine touched my lips...

What is fasting? Fasting is abstaining from something you love, as unto God. It is a Biblical habit that can help us get closer to Jesus. The first mention of Daniel's fast is in the first chapter of the book named after this prophet. Nebuchadnezzar, the king of Babylon, requested some of the smartest, best-looking, and most flawless young men of Israel to come work in the king's palace. Daniel and his companions were chosen but they refused to eat the king's delicacies. This is in the context of Israel's captivity in Babylon. They were in a foreign land and dietary laws were one of the many aspects of Jewish life that set them apart as the people of God. The king's food was considered defiled and unholy. The Bible reveals how Daniel, Shadrach, Meshach, and Abednego seemed healthier and more nourished after 10 days of eating vegetables and drinking only water. As a result, God gave these young men more wisdom than all of the astrologers and magicians of the land. The second instance of Daniel's fast happens in chapter 10 where we see that he fasted for 3 weeks, eating no meat or "choice food." In return, God blessed him with a prophetic dream as he continued serving the king, humbly and steadfast in his faith.

My prayer is that you will obtain a renewed focus on God, a healthy and nurtured body, and a fresh new start as you embark on this fasting and prayer journey. I don't know where you are in your walk with God, but wherever that may be and whatever answers you're seeking, I hope that this book provides you with some ideas that will keep you motivated. Daniel Fast foods don't have to be bland and unappealing. Get the kids involved and make it a positive experience for everyone by using spices and herbs and being creative. Abstain from complaining about your fast and pray for God to fill you with strength and perseverance. Remember how the Israelites constantly grumbled about the manna, food from heaven? Let's do the opposite of that. Focus on the blessings in order to keep a positive attitude throughout the entire journey. Encourage each other and pray for one another.

This book is meant to be a resource. However, use your best, Biblical judgment and check with your pastor if you are unsure about something. For instance, if using vinegar in your salad dressings goes against your guidelines and convictions, then lemon juice is a good, natural alternative. However, I don't know too many people who would indulge in vinegar. So I don't worry too much if not all the ingredients fit perfectly within every guideline you find online. Realistically speaking, if you're not a vegan already, you will miss going out to eat juicy steaks and cheesy pizza. Fasting is personal. It may not be a big deal for me to give up beef for a month, but it may be a huge sacrifice for someone else. What really matters is where your heart is. Fasting is sacrificing unto Jesus to grow closer to Him.

## WHAT'S IN SEASON?

After all the Christmas feasting and splurging on delicious foods and desserts, it seems like January, by far, is the official Daniel Fast month. Consider using seasonal vegetables and fruits in your dishes. You'll get sweeter, richer flavors and you'll also get more for your money. Find out what's available in your area. Try fasting during the summer months when most vegetables and fruits are in season.

## CLEAN EATING

Have you ever heard the saying, "You are what you eat?" The Daniel Fast is a great opportunity to detox and improve your overall health. Eat lots of fresh fruits, vegetables, and unprocessed whole grains. Your goal is to have 100% natural foods.

# THE GUIDELINES
## WHAT WOULD DANIEL EAT TODAY...IF HE LIVED IN YOUR HOUSE

WHAT TO EAT:

All fruits and vegetables

All legumes (beans and lentils, etc)

Whole grains (whole wheat, oatmeal, barley, corn, brown rice, etc)

Whole grain flat breads

Sugar-free whole grain cereals

Nuts and seeds

Tofu

Herbs and spices

WHAT TO DRINK:

Water and 100% fruit and vegetable juices, preferably homemade

WHAT TO AVOID:

Pleasant Foods, Meat, and Wine would probably include, but not be limited to:

Anything derived from an animal (meat, poultry, eggs, dairy, cheese, bacon, butter, seafood, etc).

Sugar

Caffeine

Highly processed foods and preservatives

Artificially flavored drinks and snacks

Carbonated and energy drinks

Chocolate

Fried foods

Bread (French bread, dinner rolls, etc)

Wine and alcohol

WHAT ABOUT FERMENTED FOODS? Some Daniel Fast guidelines suggest avoiding fermented foods like soy sauce, tofu, and vinegar. Even though these are not necessarily super pleasant foods, in my opinion, it is always best to avoid processed foods that are high in sodium and preservatives. Read the labels and make careful choices. Bragg Liquid Aminos is a non-fermented soy sauce which works great in stir-fries.

Always check with your doctor to make sure this fast is safe for you.

CHOICES: Daniel's food options might have been more limited compared to the vast array of food choices we have available today, considering we live in a global economy. So, you may not live in ancient Babylon to eat exactly what Daniel ate, but we do have more choices of what we can eat. The main concept of the Daniel fast is to avoid fun foods and meat. It's a humbling experience because you won't be eating like a king.

Powerhouse Zucchini Loaf p. 17

# BREAKFAST AND SNACKS

# daniel fast cookies

YOU NEED:

- 1 cup whole wheat flour
- 1 teaspoon baking powder
- 1/4 teaspoon sea salt
- 1 cup rolled or steel cut oats
- 1/2 teaspoon cinnamon
- 1/2 teaspoon ground allspice
- 1/2 cup grated carrots
- 1/2 cup agave
- 1/4 cup grape seed oil
- 1/2 cup chopped nuts
- 1/2 cup dried berry medley

Don't want to use agave? Try blending dates and water to create a caramely syrup for baking. Simply soak about a dozen medjool dates in 1 1/2 cups of warm water for 30 minutes. Blend until smooth.

STEP-BY-STEP:

1. Preheat oven to 375F degrees and line two flat metal baking sheets with parchment paper.

2. In a large bowl, whisk together all dry ingredients, flour, and spices.

3. In a separate bowl, combine all liquid ingredients and grated carrots.

4. Slowly add the flour mixture to the the wet ingredients. Mix well.

5. Drop onto prepared baking sheets, one level tablespoonful or ice cream scoop at a time, leaving about 2 inches of space between each cookie.

6. Bake for 10 - 12 minutes or until the cookies are golden on top and bottom. For best results, bake on the top level rack of your oven.

Makes about 2 dozen cookies.

*Baking powder is optional in this recipe.

# blueberry pancakes

YOU NEED:

- 1 cup whole wheat flour

- pinch of salt

- 1 cup almond or soy milk

- 1/4 cup apple sauce

- grape seed or olive oil

- 1/4 cup agave syrup

- 1/2 cup frozen blueberries

Try adding some grated apples or pears, chopped bananas, and/or strawberries to the batter.

STEP-BY-STEP:

1. Mix flour, milk, apple sauce, pinch of salt, and one tablespoon of oil. The mixture will be kind of lumpy.

2. Sprinkle in 1/4 cup of blueberries and stir.

3. Heat about a teaspoon of oil on a non-stick pan or griddle on medium heat. You can use non-stick spray instead of oil.

4. Pour about a 1/4 cup of batter on the pan and spread it evenly with the back of a ladle, forming a circle. This is an important step. If you make these pancakes too thick, they might fall apart when you try to flip them, plus the blueberries make the mixture heavier and really moist. Add more oil to the pan if necessary after each pancake.

5. Allow pancakes to get bubbly and almost dry on top before you flip them. Because the mixture doesn't have any baking powder, these pancakes are not going to be fluffy and doughy. They are kind of thin and crêpe-like.

6. Combine remaining agave and blueberries and microwave for 30 secs. Lightly drizzle blueberry syrup over pancakes.

Makes about 6 pancakes.

And God said, "See, I have given you every herb that yields seed which is on the face of all the earth, and every tree whose fruit yields seed; to you it shall be for food."

Genesis 1:29

# easy oaty berry crumble

Here's a sweet and crunchy topping
for your oatmeal or cream of wheat.

YOU NEED:

- 2 cups frozen or fresh berries (blueberries, black berries, cranberries, etc)

- 1 teaspoon cinnamon

- 1/4 teaspoon nutmeg

- 1/4 cup plain oatmeal

- 1/4 cup Ezekiel 4:9 Original Crunchy Cereal

- 1 tablespoon wheat germ (optional)

- 5 tablespoons whole wheat flour

- 2 or 3 tbs agave syrup

- 1/4 cup chopped nuts

- grape seed or olive oil

STEP-BY-STEP:

1. Preheat oven to 350F and spray a baking dish with non-stick spray.

2. In a bowl, sprinkle the berries with 1 tablespoon of flour, 1 tablespoon of agave syrup, and spices. Mix well and pour into baking dish, evenly spreading the mixture.

3. In a separate bowl, combine oats, cereal, wheat germ, 4 tablespoons of flour, and nuts.

4. Next, gradually drizzle a couple tablespoons of oil and agave until the mixture is crumbly. Evenly layer the oat mixture on top of berries.

5. Bake for about 25 minutes.

arroz con leche

Rice pudding is simple comfort food. When I was little, I loved making rice pudding with my mom. It was one of my favorite desserts. Just thinking about it takes me back to warm, childhood memories.

## YOU NEED:

- 4 cups water

- 1 cinnamon stick

- 1 cup brown rice

- 1 pinch of salt

- 4 cups almond milk

- 4 tablespoons agave syrup (optional)

- 1 teaspoon vanilla extract

- 1/2 cup dried fruit (raisins, cranberries, etc)

- cinnamon powder

## STEP-BY-STEP:

1. First, boil 4 cups of water with the cinnamon stick. Add the brown rice and salt. Simmer uncovered for 30 minutes or until the rice is tender, stirring occasionally. The rice will be deliciously infused with a wonderful cinnamon flavor.

2. Drain your rice. You don't need to rinse it because the starch will help give the pudding a thick, creamy consistency and that's exactly what you want. The cinnamon stick can be left in the rice and removed before serving.

3. Return the rice to the pot you cooked it in and add the almond milk, agave, and vanilla. Bring to a very low simmer, stirring often so nothing burns or sticks to the bottom of the pot. Simmer for about 15–30 minutes, depending on how tender your want the rice. Brown rice requires more cooking time than white rice.

4. You can mix in some dried fruit while it's cooking but I prefer to add it as a garnish at the end. You can serve this warm for breakfast, at room temperature, or cold as a dessert. Sprinkle some powdered cinnamon on it before serving.

# breakfast energy wrap

Spices can make your Daniel Fast dishes a little more flavorful and interesting. Sprinkle cinnamon on bananas and get an immediate burst of flavor.

## YOU NEED:

- 1 whole grain tortilla
- 2 tablespoons peanut or almond butter
- 1/2 banana, sliced
- 1 handful berries (ex. blueberries, raspberries, etc)
- sliced almonds or crushed walnuts to sprinkle on top (cereal or peanuts would work too)
- ground cinnamon (optional)
- agave syrup (optional)

## STEP-BY-STEP:

1. Lightly spread about two tablespoons of peanut butter on the tortilla.

2. Spread banana slices on top of the peanut butter. Sprinkle some berries, nuts, and add a few dashes of cinnamon.

3. Lightly drizzle some agave syrup over all the ingredients if you want more sweetness. This is optional as sugar, in all shapes and forms, should be limited during the Daniel Fast.

4. Roll up the tortilla into a wrap or burrito. Take it to-go as you head out to work. It makes a great after-school snack, too!

# yams in orange syrup

YOU NEED:

- 2 medium sized yams (the large ones are often too ripe for this recipe)

- 2 cinnamon sticks

- 1 cup freshly squeezed orange juice

- 1 long curl of orange peel

- 1 teaspoon whole cloves

- agave syrup (optional)

These fragrant and citrusy yams are so delicious on pancakes or oatmeal for breakfast. They will remind you of fall and winter. Oranges add a zesty freshness and natural sweetness to salads and baked goods.

My inspiration for this recipe was "camotes en miel," a syrupy yam dessert from El Salvador, which is where I was born.

STEP-BY-STEP:

1. Preheat your oven to 425F.

2. Peel, cube, and rinse yams.

3. Place them in a baking dish along with the cinnamon sticks and orange peel studded with cloves (this makes it easy to remove them at the end).

4. Sprinkle with some agave syrup and pour the orange juice over the yams.

5. Bake for 30 minutes covered with foil.

6. Uncover, then bake for an additional 10-15 minutes or until slightly brown and tender.

7. Sprinkle with some cinnamon powder. Serve warm or cold.

Note: You can parboil yams before baking. This will slash the baking time in half. The same goes for other root vegetables like carrots, beets, and potatoes.

# banana split

**YOU NEED:**

- 1 banana

- 1 tablespoon nut butter (peanut, almond, etc.)

- 1 tablespoon ground flax seeds or wheat germ

- 1 tablespoon chopped nuts

- 1/4 cup of whole grain Daniel-Fast-friendly cereal such as Ezekiel, Weetabix, etc.

- 1/2 cup berries, fresh or frozen and somewhat thawed

- 1 tablespoon agave syrup, optional

- vanilla-flavored soy or almond milk, optional

**STEP-BY-STEP:**

1. Cut banana in half lengthwise.

2. Spread nut butter on each banana half and gently press them together like a sandwich.

3. Sprinkle banana with ground flax, pecans and cereal. Top with berries and a little drizzle of agave.

4. Add a splash of really cold, non-dairy milk and enjoy.

> Taste and see that the Lord is good; blessed is the man that takes refuge in him.
>
> Psalms 34:8

# powerhouse zucchini loaf

## YOU NEED:

- 1 1/2 cups wholewheat flour
- 1/3 cup of oatmeal
- 1/2 teaspoon salt
- 1/2 teaspoon baking soda
- 1/4 teaspoon baking powder
- 1 teaspoon cinnamon
- 1 cup finely grated zucchini
- 1 cup apple sauce
- 1 very ripe mashed banana or plantain
- 1/3 cup vegetable or grape seed oil
- 1 teaspoon vanilla extract
- 3 tablespoons of agave syrup (optional)
- 1/2 cup chopped nuts

## STEP-BY-STEP:

1. Preheat the oven to 350F. Using a brush, lightly grease a loaf baking dish with oil or vegan margarine. Set aside.

2. Mix all the dry ingredients together, except the nuts, in a large mixing bowl. Set aside.

3. Next, in another large mixing bowl, combine the wet ingredients, including the zucchini, mixing constantly to meld all the flavors together. The mixture will be very wet and lumpy.

4. Gently add the dry ingredients to the wet ingredients and mix until well combined. Fold in the nuts at the end.

5. Pour the batter into the baking dish. Optional: sprinkle a handful of crumbled cereal like Shredded Wheat, Cornflakes, or Weetabix on top of the batter to add some extra crunch.

6. Bake for 50 minutes, or until the bread is golden brown and a toothpick or knife comes out clean when inserted into the center of the bread.

7. Cool completely before serving.

# baked stuffed apples

YOU NEED:

- 6 medium apples (any kind of apples)

- 3 tablespoons grape seed or olive oil

- 4 tablespoons agave syrup (optional)

- 1/4 teaspoon nutmeg

- 1/4 teaspoon ground cinnamon

- 1/2 cup chopped nuts

- 1/2 cup whole wheat flour

- 1/4 cup oatmeal

- 1/4 cup Ezekiel 4:9 Original Crunchy Cereal

- 1/4 cup wheat germ or ground flax seed (optional)

- 1 slice of lemon (optional)

STEP-BY-STEP:

1. Preheat oven to 425F.

2. Cut the apples in half lengthwise, remove the cores, and hollow out apples with an ice cream scoop, paring knife, or spoon.

3. Trim a thin slice off the back of each apple half so they sit flat on a baking dish.

4. Rub tops of apples with lemon to prevent browning. This is optional since apples will brown in the oven. If you're planning to make these in advance and bake later, than definitely use lemon to prevent oxidation.

5. Combine oil and agave syrup in a bowl, then add all the dry ingredients and spices. The mixture will be crumbly. Granola also works great as a filling for apples.

6. Pack this mixture into apples and place in a shallow baking dish, lined with parchment paper. Bake for 17-20 minutes or until the apples are tender but not too soft. Drizzle with agave syrup if desired.

# pumpkin apple muffins

YOU NEED:

- 1 cup oats, any kind
- 1 cup wholewheat flour
- 1 teaspoon cinnamon
- 1 teaspoon pumpkin spice
- 1 teaspoon baking soda (optional)
- 1 cup pumpkin purée
- 1 cup apple sauce
- 1/2 cup agave syrup
- 1/4 cup grape seed oil
- 1 cup finely diced apples

STEP–BY–STEP:

1. Preheat oven to 350F.

2. Mix dry ingredients together in a large bowl.

The muffins shown on this page do not have any baking soda, which is optional, depending on the guidelines you're following. Without the rising agent, the muffins will have a less bread–like texture and be more moist and crumbly... absolutely delicious with a hot cup of cinnamon tea.

3. In another bowl, combine wet ingredients.

4. Mix wet and dry ingredients into a smooth paste. Add apples and continue to mix until all the ingredients are well incorporated.

5. Scoop mixture into muffin tin lined with paper baking cups. Feel free to fill cups completely if you're not using any baking soda.

6. Bake for 25 min.

# carrot bliss juice

This is my daughter's favorite juice. She started drinking it when she was an infant and continues loving it as a toddler. The great thing about juicing is that you can "conceal" the flavor of veggies by letting the juicer crush them together with ripe, yummy fruit. The fruit flavors will overpower the concoction and result in a drinkable glass of pure fuel for the mind and body. A good trick to know if you got picky eaters.

YOU NEED:
• about 15 carrots

• 1 zucchini

• 2 pears

OPTIONAL GARNISH:
• chopped fruit of your choice

STEP-BY STEP:

1.Pass the carrots, zucchini, and pears through a juice maker, according to manufacturer's directions.

2.Serve chilled or pour over ice. Garnish with diced fruit.

Makes about 2 glasses of juice.

GOOD TO KNOW: If you're craving a good beverage during your Daniel Fast, drink homemade juice. Many store-bought juices are highly processed and may contain more sugar than nutrients. Therefore, a juicer is a really good investment you won't regret.

# datelicious coconut ice cream

YOU NEED:

- 2 cans full fat coconut milk

- 2 cups unpacked Medjool dates, pitted and roughly chopped

- 2 teaspoons vanilla extract

GARNISH:

- chopped almonds, peanuts, or walnuts

Dates are a staple food in the Middle East and are mentioned more than 50 times in the Bible. With that said, wait until you taste this ice cream. I'm glad my husband came up with this amazing idea.

STEP-BY-STEP:

1. In a pot over medium heat, combine coconut milk, dates, and vanilla.

2. Simmer for 10 minutes, stirring constantly, until mixture thickens up and dates are soft.

3. Remove from the heat and allow to cool for at least 15 minutes.

4. Blend well and strain if desired.

5. Refrigerate for at least 5 hours or overnight.

6. Pour mixture into ice cream maker and churn for 20 minutes. See manufacturer's instructions.

Latin Inspired Bean Soup, p. 43

# LUNCH AND DINNER

# pasta e fagioli

TIP: Canned beans and vegetable broth are essential staples during the Daniel Fast. Make comforting and satisfying soups in less than 30 minutes by always having these on hand. Of course, if you're trying to save a few bucks, use water instead of vegetable stock. You'll still get pretty tasty results.

YOU NEED:

- 1 cup whole grain or whole wheat elbow macaroni

- 1 tablespoon grape seed or olive oil

- 1 cup chopped onion

- 1 minced or pressed garlic clove

- 1 carrot, diced

- 1 red or yellow bell pepper

- couple of fresh thyme and rosemary sprigs (substitute Italian seasoning)

- 1 bay leaf

- 2 (32-ounce) cartons low sodium vegetable broth

- 1 can white kidney beans, drained (use 2 cans of beans if you decide to leave out the meat substitute)

- 1 package meat substitute (optional)

- pinch red pepper flakes (optional)

- 1 can diced tomatoes (optional)

- chopped kale to garnish

- salt and pepper to taste

STEP-BY-STEP:

1. Cook pasta and set aside.

2. Heat the oil in a pot, add the onions, carrots, bell peppers, garlic and sauté until the onion is tender, which should take about 3-5 minutes.

3. Add the rest of the ingredients, except the kale. Cover and bring to a boil over high heat, then decrease the heat to medium-low and simmer for 10 minutes until the veggies are tender.

4. Add the pasta, ladle the soup into bowls, and garnish with raw kale.

Note: What isn't there to love about pasta and beans?! You can enhance the flavor of this soup with just about any seasonal vegetable and herbs you have on hand. It's hearty and warming, perfect during winter.

On busy days, I prefer to use frozen stir-fry vegetables. Now, that's easy!

Maifun noodles resemble vermicelli noodles or angel hair pasta and can be found in the Asian foods aisle at your local grocery or whole foods store.

# maifun noodle stir fry

MEASURE-FREE RECIPE

## YOU NEED:

- 1 package maifun brown rice noodles
- sesame oil
- garlic, mashed
- vegetable or grape seed oil
- carrots, thinly sliced into match sticks
- sugar snap peas
- soy bean sprouts
- cabbage, thinly sliced
- low-sodium soy sauce
- vegetable broth
- salt and pepper to taste

## STEP-BY-STEP:

1. Boil or cook noodles according to package instructions.

2. Drizzle sesame oil on noodles and toss. This will prevent noodles from sticking together too much.

1. In a non-stick skillet or wok pan, heat about one tablespoon of vegetable oil over medium-high heat, add carrots and stir fry for about 30 seconds.

2. Next, add sugar snap peas, garlic, bean sprouts, and cabbage. Toss all the vegetables together and season with salt and pepper.

3. Drizzle with a little more vegetable oil, sprinkle with soy sauce and vegetable broth.

Stir fry for about 30 more seconds.

4. Stir in noodles and add a little more broth and soy sauce to keep the mixture from drying out. Cook for about 30 seconds, tossing lightly to mix all the ingredients together.

5. Serve immediately while the veggies are still crunchy.

*Yields about 6 large servings.

Option: Feel free to incorporate other vegetables like mushrooms and bell peppers. Sometimes I like to sprinkle my stir-fries with green onions, chopped cilantro, and red pepper flakes to spice up the flavor.

# daniel fast paella

YOU NEED:

- 3 tablespoons olive oil

- 1 can garbanzo beans, drained

- 1 red bell pepper, thinly sliced

- 1 medium onion, chopped

- 1 cup Spanish olives stuffed with pimentos

- salt and pepper to taste

- 1/2 teaspoon turmeric powder or saffron

- 1 teaspoon no-salt vegan seasoning

- 7 cups vegetable stock or water

- 1-2 plum tomatoes, cut in wedges

- 3 cups uncooked long grain brown rice

- 2 cups green beans, whole or long pieces

- 1 12 oz jar marinated artichoke hearts (optional)

STEP-BY-STEP:

1. Sauté onions on medium heat and stir for about 2 or 3 minutes.

2. When onions are tender and translucent, add bell peppers, garbanzos, olives, and rice and continue stirring for about 2 more minutes. Add all the seasonings to the mixture before adding the liquid.

3. Pour vegetable stock and bring to a boil.

4. Cover and simmer over low heat for about 40 minutes.

5. Add the tomatoes, green beans, and cover again. Stir gently. Continue to cook for 10-15 more minutes or until the liquid is completely absorbed. Brown rice takes longer to cook than white rice.

6. Mix in the marinated artichokes right before you're ready to eat the rice. Serve with lemon wedges.

*Don't have saffron or turmeric? No problem! These are not essential ingredients since their main purpose in this recipe is to add some color to the rice. Saffron has a mild earthy taste and has to be soaked in the cooking liquid for a few minutes before adding it to the rice. Turmeric is pretty much tasteless but it does have some medicinal properties.

TIP: This recipe serves 6-8 people and it's meant to be a meal in itself, not a side dish. If you need to make less rice, downsize to 2 cups of brown rice to 5 cups of liquid.

Extra firm tofu is the perfect source of protein to complement your stir fries and curry dishes. *Recipe courtesy of my mom, Mirna Alvarado

# easy tofu stir fry

YOU NEED:

- 1/2 lb. extra firm tofu, drained and sliced

- 1 zucchini, cut into 1/4-inch slices

- 1 Japanese eggplant, cut into 1/4-inch slices (Japanese eggplant is firmer than regular eggplant)

- 1 yellow summer squash, cut into 1/4-inch slices

- 1/2 fresh asparagus, cut into 1-inch pieces

- 1/2 onion, thinly sliced

- 2 tablespoons grape seed or sesame oil (eggplant and tofu are very absorbent so you may need a little extra oil)

- salt and pepper to taste

STEP-BY-STEP:

1. Heat oil in a pan and brown tofu for about 5 minutes on each side. Season with salt and pepper.

2. Add onions and sauté until translucent.

3. Add veggies and stir fry all the ingredients until they start browning and caramelizing nicely. Vegetables should be crispy so do not cover. Placing a lid on the pan will cause everything to steam and your tofu will be too soggy.

4. Serve immediately.

Keep soy chorizo on hand during your Daniel Fast and put together easy meals like these yummy tacos in a cinch. Try it in vegan chilli and bean soups. Mix it with potatoes, green beans, corn, and diced carrots to make burritos. The options are endless. Enjoy!

# southwest veggie tacos

## YOU NEED:

- 1 link Trader Joe's Soy Chorizo (vegan and no preservatives)

- 1/2 large onion, diced

- 1/2 large green bell pepper, diced

- 1/2 yellow or red bell pepper, diced

- 4 cloves garlic, minced or pressed (optional)

- 1 can corn, drained

- 1 can garbanzo beans, drained (same as chick peas)

- 2 tomatoes, diced

- 1 small can diced green chiles or green salsa (I like to use Trader Joe's New Mexico Valley Fire Roasted Diced Green Chile)

- chopped cilantro to garnish (optional)

- salt and pepper to taste

## STEP-BY-STEP:

1. Remove the soy chorizo from the casing and heat in a pan.

1. Use a little oil if necessary, add the rest of the ingredients and cook for about 5 minutes or until onions are translucent.

2. Add tomatoes at the end, then mix, and serve on warm tortillas.

It's that easy!

Try this delish soy chorizo mixture on tostadas and as a filling for burritos. Mix it with some rice for stuffed bell peppers or layer it on top of beans, salsa, and guacamole to create the most appetizing "I-can't-believe- it's-vegan" dip.

# fiesta pizza

YOU NEED:

- 1 package Trader Joe's whole wheat pizza dough (disclaimer: it's not unleavened)

- 1/2 cup marinara sauce

- olive oil

- non-stick spray

- cornmeal (if you have some on hand)

- shredded soy cheese (optional)

- Toppings: You can use any fresh vegetables you have in your fridge, either diced or thinly sliced. Here are some ideas: zucchini, mushrooms, corn, bell peppers, onions, tomatoes, spinach, olives, marinated or canned artichokes, crumbled veggie burgers, etc.

STEP-BY-STEP:

1. Allow dough to rest at room temperature for about an hour before using.

2. Pre-heat oven to 425F.

3. Prepare your veggies in the meantime. You can use them raw or quickly sautéed.

4. Roll out dough on a large, floured cutting board or gently spread it and stretch it out with your hands. Your pizza doesn't have to be perfectly round. I always make mine rectangular to fit on a cookie sheet. This is a thin-crust pizza.

5. Spray a baking sheet with non-stick cooking spray and sprinkle some cornmeal on it to prevent dough from sticking. Lay out dough on baking sheet and brush it with some olive oil.

6. Ladle the sauce and spread it evenly on the dough, then add the cheese and layer the toppings. Bake for 10-13 minutes.

Oven Tip: Not all ovens are created equal, so you may have to experiment with the baking time.

Consider using corn as another ingredient just like my husband does. It gives the pizza a sweet taste.

# lentil ragout

YOU NEED:

- 1/2 green bell pepper, diced

- 1 carrot, diced

- 1/2 onion, finely diced

- 1 stick of celery, diced

- 2 cloves garlic, finely diced

- 1 cup dry lentils

- 2 cans diced tomatoes

- 1 bay leaf

- 1 teaspoon dried oregano

- 1 teaspoon Italian seasoning

- grape seed oil

- 4 cups vegetable stock

- salt and freshly ground black pepper

Lentils are so versatile and super healthy. Try using pasta sauce instead of diced tomatoes, and add other veggies like mushrooms and zucchini. There is no need to worry about perfect measurements. If you're like me, an eyeball-it-sort-of-cook, then you can just imagine the possibilities!

STEP-BY-STEP:

1. Coat a sauté pan or saucepan with oil and toss in all the veggies together, along with herbs and seasonings. Sauté the mixture over medium heat for about 10 minutes. This is an important step. By browning veggies along with herbs, the flavors will be more intense.

1. Next, add lentils, diced tomatoes, and stock. Stir to remove all the bits and pieces that might have stuck to the bottom of the pot. Bring to a quick boil and reduce heat to low.

1. Simmer for about 45 minutes to an hour or until lentils are tender. Stir occasionally and pour in more stock to keep lentils from drying out.

2. Serve over whole wheat pasta or brown rice.

Going beyond hummus...

Chick peas are not just for hummus and salad bars. These versatile legumes come from the Middle East and are widely used in Mediterranean, Middle Eastern, and Indian cuisines. Garbanzos, as they are commonly known, are high in fiber and protein, making them extremely nutritious; plus they are gluten-free. Mix them into a variety of dishes like stews, soups, rice, pancakes, curries, and more! Here's a really tasty garbanzo bread recipe from Italy's Tuscan region. The French also have a version called Socca. Experiment with adding different herbs and even toppings like tomatoes and caramelized onions. Yum! This is the perfect Daniel Fast snack for your next get-together or picnic.

# farinata di ceci: chickpea flour

YOU NEED:

- 4 cups chickpea flour a.k.a. garbanzo flour

- 6 cups of water

- 8 tablespoons olive oil

- 1 tablespoon salt

- pepper to taste

- about 1 teaspoon dried herbs of your choice

- a pinch of cumin (optional)

STEP-BY-STEP:

1. In a large mixing bowl and using a whisk, mix together chickpea flour and water until the mixture is no longer lumpy and the consistency is smooth and milky.

2. Add 2 tablespoons of olive oil, herbs, salt, and pepper. Continue whisking to incorporate all the ingredients into flour mixture. Set aside and allow the mixture to rest for about an hour. This will allow the batter to thicken up a bit and allow all the flavors to meld together.

3. Preheat your oven to 450F just a few minutes before the next step. Ovens do vary so plan accordingly.

4. Spread the rest of the oil on two 14" pizza pans or cookie sheets. Pour the milky batter in the middle of each pan so that it floats in the oil. **Warning: Don't shake or tilt the pans.** Heavy duty cookie sheets may work better than pizza pans to prevent oil from dripping in the oven.

5. Bake for 30 minutes or until golden brown. This recipe yields two, huge delicious flatbreads. It's worth the effort!

# roasted garbanzos

**YOU NEED:**

- 1 can garbanzo beans/ chickpeas

- 3 tablespoons olive or grape seed oil

- 1/2 teaspoon salt

- 1/2 teaspoon freshly ground pepper

- seasoning blend of your choice (ex. chili, cajun, Italian, curry, garlic, etc. Be creative!)

**STEP-BY-STEP:**

1. Preheat oven to 400F. Rinse and drain the chickpeas well in a colander; make sure to shake the colander to remove all the excess water. Removing the lose skins is completely optional.

2. In a large bowl, combine the chickpeas with olive oil, salt, and pepper. Use your hands or a spoon to mix the ingredients together.

3. Spread the chickpeas on a baking sheet and roast for about 15 minutes or until the chickpeas begin to brown.

4. Sprinkle spices on chickpeas and shake the baking sheet a little bit to blend all the flavors together. Bake for 5-10 more minutes or until the chickpeas are golden brown and crispy. Serve immediately.

# lettuce wraps

Here's a dish you can put together in a heart beat. Use any Daniel Fast-friendly ingredients you have on hand.

YOU NEED:

- small red potatoes, cubed
- red bell pepper, diced
- tomatoes, diced
- green onions, thinly sliced
- carrots, cubed
- soy bean sprouts
- 1 package Boca soy crumbles
- grape seed oil to coat the pan
- low-sodium soy sauce or tamari sauce
- sesame seed oil
- salt and pepper to taste
- iceberg or butter lettuce, leaves separated, cleaned and dried
- Upgrades: crumbled tofu, onions, garlic, green beans, mushrooms, zucchini, frozen stir fry vegetables, corn, etc.

STEP-BY-STEP:

1. Brown potatoes in a non-stick pan on medium heat for about 15 minutes or until they're tender.
2. Stir in soy crumbles. Cook for 5 more minutes.
3. Next, mix in the rest of the veggies, except green onions. Sprinkle the mixture with some sesame oil and soy sauce.
4. Lightly sauté the veggies until they reach desired doneness. You may pour some water or vegetable stock to prevent potatoes from drying out. Season with salt and pepper.
5. Arrange lettuce leaves on a serving platter or large plate; mound veggie mixture in the center, and garnish with thinly sliced green onions. Spoon a portion of the filling into a lettuce leaf and eat like a taco.

# indian coconut curried vegetables

## YOU NEED:

- 1 turnip (or potato)

- 1 carrot (julienned or thinly sliced with a vegetable peeler)

- 1 zucchini

- 1/2 red bell pepper

- 1/2 green bell pepper

- 6 or more frozen pearl onions

- 1 garlic clove, mashed

- 1 can chick peas

- 2 tablespoons grape seed oil

- 1 pinch of cinnamon

- 2 tablespoons of curry powder

- salt and pepper to taste

- 1/2 can diced tomatoes (you can definitely use fresh tomatoes)

- 1/2 can light coconut milk

- 1 bunch of cilantro, chopped

## STEP-BY-STEP:

1. Heat the oil in pan on medium-high heat.

2. Sauté all the veggies and chick peas, except the tomatoes. Add mashed garlic clove.

3. Season veggies with curry powder, a pinch of cinnamon, and salt and pepper to taste.

4. Sauté vegetables for about 3 minutes on medium-low heat.

5. Add tomatoes and simmer on low heat for 20-30 more minutes or until vegetables reach desired doneness.

6. Just before serving, add coconut milk and stir. Cook for 3 more minutes.

7. Serve over brown rice and sprinkle with chopped cilantro. Brown basmati rice goes perfectly with this dish. Makes about 6 servings.

# zesty salsa pasta salad

YOU NEED:

- 2 cups whole grain elbow pasta (or any bite sized pasta)

- 1 onion, chopped (green onions or red onions are preferred)

- 1 red or yellow bell pepper, diced

- 1 can kidney beans

- 1 (6 ounce) can sliced black olives

- 3 tomatoes, diced

- 2 fresh jalapeños, chopped (optional)

- chopped fresh cilantro, desired quantity

- 1 jar hearts of palm, sliced (optional)

- 1 jar baby corn, sliced (optional)

- 3/4 cup Kraft Zesty Italian dressing (make your own natural dressing by whisking together oil and lemon juice, about 1/4 cup of each)

- 1 tablespoon chili powder

- salt and pepper to taste

STEP-BY-STEP:

1. Cook pasta al dente, according to package instructions.

2. Combine all the ingredients in a large bowl. Season with salt, pepper, and chili powder. Mix well, and voila! Get ready for an explosion of flavors.

> But when you fast, comb your hair and wash your face. Then no one will notice that you are fasting, except your Father, who knows what you do in private. And your Father, who sees everything, will reward you.
>
> Matthew 6:17–18

# southwest stuffed tomatoes

MEASURE-FREE RECIPE

YOU NEED:

- salad tomatoes
- onions, chopped
- bell pepper, diced
- meat substitute or soy chorizo (optional)
- chopped mushrooms
- cooked brown rice
- canned or frozen corn
- chopped cilantro or parsley
- chili powder
- salt & pepper to taste
- grape seed oil

STEP-BY-STEP:

1. Preheat oven to 350F.

2. Cut off and discard tops of tomatoes. Scoop out seeds and pulp with a spoon. You can save the pulp and make salsa with it later.

3. Sauté meat substitute, mushrooms, onions and bell peppers. Combine this mixture with rice, corn, and cilantro.

4. Season with chili powder, salt, and pepper. Add some of the tomato pulp to the mixture to add extra moisture and mix well.

5. Fill tomato cups with the rice mixture, then place them in a baking dish and drizzle them with some oil. Bake for 20 minutes.

6. Serve these juicy stuffed tomatoes on their own or with a side of polenta.

Other Ideas: There are many versions of stuffed tomatoes such as Italian, Greek, Persian, Mexican, etc. Experiment with different herbs and seasonings to create tasty vegan versions of dishes your family loves.

# italian rice stuffed bell peppers

YOU NEED:

- 8 green, yellow, orange, or red bell peppers

- 1/2 cup onions, chopped

- 1 celery stalk, chopped

- 1/2 cup carrots, diced

- 2 cups cooked brown rice (left-over rice works great in this recipe)

- 1 teaspoon Italian seasoning

- grape seed oil

STEP-BY-STEP:

1. Preheat oven to 350F.

2. Remove tops and seeds from peppers.

3. Sauté onions, celery, and carrots for about 5 minutes.

4. Combine cooked rice and veggie mixture. Add Italian seasoning, plus salt and pepper. Mix well.

5. Remove from heat and allow mixture to cool a little bit before stuffing the peppers.

5. Use a spoon to stuff each bell pepper with rice mixture.

6. Place stuffed bell peppers in a baking dish and drizzle with some grape seed oil. Bake for 40-50 minutes. Enjoy!

Yes, everything else is worthless when compared with the infinite value of knowing Christ Jesus my Lord. For his sake I have discarded everything else, counting it all as garbage, so that I could gain Christ...

Philippians 3:8

# pinto beans in a crock pot

YOU NEED:

- 2 cups dry pinto beans, cleaned

- about 7 cups of water

- 2 whole garlic cloves

- 1 onion, quartered

- 1 green bell pepper, chopped into big pieces

- salt and pepper to taste

STEP-BY-STEP:

1. Put beans in the crock pot and add enough water to cover beans by about 2 inches. It is important that beans do not dry out, so add more water if needed.

2. Add garlic cloves, onion, and bell pepper, plus a generous pinch of salt and some freshly ground pepper.

3. Turn crock pot to HIGH and let beans cook until they're tender, about 5-6 hours or 7-8 hours on LOW.

4. Drain beans and discard garlic, onions, and bell pepper, or if making refried beans on p. 39, it is ok to blend everything together.

5. Two cups of dried beans will make about 6 cups of cooked beans. Cooked beans can be stored in the fridge in an airtight container for about a week, and can be frozen for a couple of months.

## YOU NEED:

- corn tortillas

- olive oil or olive oil spray

- refried beans

- shredded lettuce

- diced tomatoes

- salsa (see salsa recipe on p. 45)

- avocado or guacamole

## STEP-BY-STEP:

1. Preheat oven to 350F. Spray or brush each tortilla with olive oil. Place tortillas on cookie sheet in a single layer and bake for about 15 minutes, turning them once, until crispy.

2. To assemble your tostada, spread a layer of beans on the crispy tortilla. Top with lettuce, tomatoes, salsa and avocado.

## EASY AND HEALTHY REFRIED BEANS, SALVADORIAN-STYLE:

# vegan tostadas & refried beans
MEASURE-FREE RECIPE

Natural baked tostadas are available now in some stores.

To make healthy and flavorful refried beans, sauté about **1/4 of an onion**, chopped in big pieces, in a **tablespoon of oil** until translucent and slightly brown. Make sure you cook onions and beans over low medium heat to prevent oil and beans from splattering all over the place. Next, blend **3 cups of cooked pinto beans** (Central American or Peruvian beans are yummy too!). Discard onion pieces and add blended beans to the onion-infused oil. Season with salt and pepper and cook beans until bubbly. To thicken up beans, cook longer on low heat, stirring occasionally. You don't want your beans to be runny, or they won't stay on the tostadas.

# soba noodle stir fry

## YOU NEED:

- 1 package buckwheat soba noodles

- grape seed oil

- 1/2 cup broccoli

- 1/2 cup cauliflower

- 3 carrots, peeled and sliced with vegetable peeler or cut into matchsticks

- 1 bell pepper (green, yellow, red, or orange)

- 3/4 cups thinly sliced cabbage

- 3 stalks of celery, thinly sliced

- 1/2 cup mushrooms, sliced

- 1 large tomato, quartered

- 1 red or white onion, thinly sliced

- 1 garlic clove, minced or mashed

- 1 cup soybean sprouts

- salt and pepper to taste

- vegetable stock (as needed)

- red pepper flakes (optional)

- low-sodium soy sauce

- sesame oil

## STEP-BY-STEP:

1. The first thing to do when making stir-fries is to prep the vegetables. The process is quick and easy when you have all your ingredients ready to go! So start by slicing all the veggies, into thin matchsticks. Roughly chop broccoli and cauliflower into florets.

2. Prepare noodles according to package instructions and set aside. Word of caution: soba noodles taste better when cooked al dente.

3. Next, heat pan or wok over medium-high heat, and add a little bit of oil. Stir fry broccoli, cauliflower, and carrots. You can add a little vegetable stock to create some steam which helps prevent vegetables from burning or sticking to the pan.

4. Add the next layer of bell peppers, cabbage, celery, and zucchini. Sauté for about 3 minutes.

5. Stir in and sauté mushrooms, onions, soybean sprouts, tomatoes and garlic. At this point, vegetables do not need too much cooking. They should be nice and crunchy.

6. Sprinkle a little soy or tamari sauce, pepper flakes, and salt and pepper to taste. Mix well.

7. Finally, add noodles. For extra flavor and depth, drizzle a little sesame oil over the entire medley and toss together.

# ribollita: italian peasant soup

YOU NEED:

- 1 teaspoon grape seed oil

- onion, desired amount

- 1 garlic clove, mashed

- 2 unpeeled carrots, sliced

- 1 stick celery, sliced or diced

- 1 zucchini, diced

- 1 bay leaf

- salt and pepper to taste

- dried oregano or Italian herbs

- 1 tomato, roughly chopped

- 1 can cannelloni or white beans (undrained)

- 4 cups vegetable stock or water (vegetable stock adds more flavor)

- 1 package potato and whole wheat gnocchi (these are Italian potato dumplings), or use 2 medium potatoes instead (optional)

- kale, torn by hand into pieces (spinach works too)

- day-old sprouted grain bread torn in pieces

So, whether you eat or drink, or whatever
you do, do all to the glory of God.
1 Corinthians 10:31

STEP-BY-STEP:

1. Heat oil in a pot over medium-high heat and sauté onions, garlic, carrots, celery, and zucchini. Season with salt, pepper and spices. Cook for about five minutes stirring continually.

2. Add the chopped tomato, canned beans, and vegetable stock. Bring to a boil.

3. If using gnocchi, add to soup now. They'll be ready when they rise to the top.

4. Turn off the heat, and stir in kale and bread right before serving.

Serves 4-5.

# easy "meat" and potatoes

YOU NEED:

• 1/2 onion, chopped

• 1 clove of garlic, minced or mashed

• 4–6 large red potatoes, unpeeled and diced

• 1 small green bell pepper, diced

• 1/2 lb. soy meat substitute, crumbled veggie burgers, or soy chorizo (make sure it's vegan; some meat substitutes contain eggs and other mysterious ingredients)

• 1 teaspoon chili powder (season according to desired flavor)

• 1 bay leaf

• 1 teaspoon grape seed oil

• salt and pepper to taste


STEP-BY-STEP:

1. Sauté onions and garlic until the onion becomes translucent.

2. Add meat substitute and brown for 5 minutes.

3. Add bell pepper, potatoes, and all the spices. Season with salt and pepper.

4. Reduce heat to low and cook for about 30 minutes, stirring occasionally. You can add a little vegetable stock if potatoes get too dry.

# latin inspired bean soup

YOU NEED:

- 1/2 cup yellow onion, finely diced

- 1 mashed garlic clove

- 2 small red potatoes, diced

- 1 carrot, diced

- 1 plum tomato, diced

- 1 small bell pepper, diced

- 1 chayote squash, diced

- 1/4 cabbage, chopped

- 1/2 zucchini, diced

- 2 cups cooked pinto beans

- 2 cups water or vegetable broth

- salt and pepper to taste

- 1 bay leaf

- 1/2 teaspoon oregano

TOPPING OPTIONS:

- diced avocado

- chopped cilantro/onion/jalapeño mix

- fresh salsa

STEP-BY-STEP:

1. In a pot, begin by sautéing onions and garlic for a couple of minutes over medium-high heat. Season with salt and pepper.

2. Next, add all the vegetables and continue to sauté the ingredients for a few more minutes, not allowing the vegetables to overcook.

3. Blend 1 1/2 cups of the pinto beans. Reserve 1/2 cup of whole beans to add to the soup later.

4. Add blended beans to vegetable mixture. Next, add 1/2 cup of whole beans and water. Season with a little more salt and pepper if necessary, then add the bay leaf and oregano. Crush the oregano to release flavors.

5. Bring soup to a quick boil, stirring occasionally. Make sure the potatoes are soft and serve the soup topped with fresh avocado or any topping of your choice.

# leek, potato, & artichoke soup

YOU NEED:

- 2 leeks, cleaned and sliced

- 1 garlic clove, mashed

- 1 small carrot, cubed

- 2 small red potatoes, cubed

- 2 or 3 artichoke hearts, cleaned and sliced

- 3 cups vegetable broth or water

- 1/4 teaspoon organic no-salt seasoning (a blend of spices and vegetables)

- 1 handful frozen peas (optional)

- salt and pepper to taste

- 1 teaspoon grape seed oil

STEP-BY-STEP:

1. Clean and prep all the veggies.

2. Sauté leeks and garlic for a couple of minutes, and then add carrots, potatoes, and artichokes. Season with salt and pepper.

3. Brown all the vegetables. Overall, the leeks and garlic will make the soup very flavorful. Overpowering herbs won't be necessary. A little bit of no-salt seasoning is all you need.

4. Add vegetable broth and bring to a quick boil.

5. Cover, reduce to a simmer, and cook for about 30 minutes or until artichokes are tender. The potatoes will melt and thicken up your soup.

6. Add a handful of frozen peas at the last minute.

Yields 2 large servings.

This artichoke soup is hearty, satisfying, and so simple to make. It's perfect and comforting on a rainy day. Daniel would have gone back for seconds. Don't be surprised if you do! The blend of artichokes and potatoes make it smooth and filling. The subtle taste of leeks adds a flavorful background to the entire soup.

# potato tacos and salsa

YOU NEED:

- for the filling, use "Meat & Potatoes" recipe on p. 42

- 15 corn tortillas

- salsa

- grape seed oil

STEP-BY-STEP:

1. Preheat oven to 350F.

2. Microwave stack of 15 tortillas wrapped in a clean kitchen towel for 3 minutes to make them pliable. Cooking times will vary depending on your microwave and how many tortillas you need to heat.

3. Brush both sides of each tortilla with oil.

4. Put a couple tablespoons of filling on each tortilla and roll them up. Secure with toothpicks if necessary.

5. Place tacos on a baking sheet and bake for about 10 minutes. If they are not crispy enough, bake them for 5 more minutes or until they reach desired crispiness.

4. Serve with shredded lettuce and salsa.

VERY BASIC SALSA:

- 1 large tomato

- 1 jalapeño or 3 dried chiles de arbol (use green bell pepper if you don't like spicy salsa)

- 1/4 onion (optional)

- chopped cilantro (optional)

- salt to taste

STEP-BY-STEP:

1. Boil the ingredients in water, except cilantro, in a sauce pan for 5 minutes.

2. Blend and season with a little salt. Add chopped cilantro and mix well.

*Warning: It's a little spicy.

# polenta

## YOU NEED:

- 3 cups water
- 1/2 teaspoon salt
- 3 tablespoons olive oil, plus more if grilling
- 1 cup Bob's Red Mill Polenta

## SAUCES AND TOPPINGS:

- Marinara sauce
- Vegan chili
- Berry syrup

## STEP-BY-STEP:

1. Boil the water, salt, and 1 tablespoon of oil in a non-stick sauce pot.

2. Gradually add polenta and reduce heat to low. Simmer gently and stir constantly to prevent sticking.

3. Add desired seasonings depending on your choice of flavor.

4. Continue cooking for about 5–7 minutes until the mixture thickens up and feels kind of like mashed potatoes but more dense. Make sure to use a long-handled spoon because the polenta bubbles like lava and it's really hot!

5. Pour polenta into a well-oiled spring form pan or baking dish; cover with plastic wrap and refrigerate until the mixture sets and cools completely. This can be done overnight. Serve as is or grilled.

5. To grill, remove polenta from the pan or baking dish, and cut into triangles or circles. Lightly oil a grill pan and sear polenta on each side for about 3 minutes on medium-high heat, until golden. Serve with topping of your choice.

This simple, yet, flavorful meal can be made in about 30 minutes. No oven required. Just pour the warm sauce over the filled tortillas and dinner is ready!

# quick mole enchiladas

## YOU NEED:

- 6 small red potatoes, diced
- 1/4 or 1/2 onion, chopped
- 1 bell pepper, chopped
- 2 tablespoons extra-virgin olive oil
- 1 generous cup cooked pinto beans
- 3 dried pasilla or California chiles, deseeded
- 2 cups vegetable broth
- 1 small tomato
- 1 tablespoon peanut butter
- 1 teaspoon dried oregano
- 1/2 teaspoon chili powder
- salt and pepper to taste
- 11 tortillas

## STEP-BY-STEP:

1. For the filling: sauté potatoes, 1/2 bell pepper, and onions in a little oil on medium-high heat. Season with salt, pepper, and sprinkle with a little chili powder. Stir occasionally.

2. Cook the potatoes until tender, for about 10 minutes. In a food processor, combine potato mixture and cooked beans. Pulse a few times until all ingredients are combined. You can use a potato masher instead of a food processor. Set mixture aside.

3. For the sauce: While the potatoes cook, soak the deseeded dried peppers in hot water to reconstitute them. Set aside. In the meantime, toast 1 tortilla on a gas stove burner. Tear into pieces and set aside. If you don't have a gas stove, use a grill pan or toaster. A handful of tortilla chips will also do the trick.

4. Next, blend together soaked peppers, 1 toasted tortilla, 1/2 bell pepper, tomato, peanut butter, vegetable broth, oregano, and 1/2 teaspoon of chili powder. Blend until the sauce is very smooth.

5. Pour the sauce in the pan where you cooked the potatoes, and add salt and pepper to taste. Simmer and reduce sauce for about 10 minutes on medium low-heat.

6. To assemble enchiladas: heat a stack of 10 tortillas wrapped in a clean kitchen towel in the microwave for 1 1/2- 2 minutes so they become pliable and easy to roll. Allow tortillas to cool for a minute, and then place about 2 tablespoons of potato filling in the middle of each tortilla. Roll into tacos and pour the simmering sauce over the rolled tortillas. Garnish with a little chopped cilantro.

# mediterranean rice salad

## MEASURE–FREE RECIPE

YOU NEED:

- cooked brown rice

- cherry tomatoes

- marinated or canned artichokes, drained

- green bell pepper, diced

- canned sliced black olives, drained

- green onions, thinly sliced (optional)

- capers, drained (optional)

- lemon juice (if needed)

- grape seed oil (if needed)

- chopped parsley (optional)

- salt and pepper to taste

> And I tell you, ask, and it will be given to you; seek, and you will find; knock, and it will be opened to you.
>
> Luke 11:9

STEP–BY–STEP:

1. Cut cherry tomatoes in half and dice or slice onions and bell peppers.

2. Mix rice and vegetables in a bowl.

3. Mix together three parts oil for every one part lemon juice to make a dressing. When I make this, it seems like the oil and acidity from the marinated artichokes is more than plenty so I don't need to make a dressing.

4. Season with freshly ground pepper and add salt if needed. Mix well and serve. It even tastes better when chilled overnight.

# baked sweet potato "fries"

## MEASURE-FREE RECIPE

YOU NEED:

- sweet potatoes, unpeeled and sliced into long slices

- splash of olive oil

- dash of salt-free vegan seasoning

- salt and pepper to taste

STEP-BY-STEP:

1. Preheat the oven to 425F.

2. Toss the sweet potatoes with olive oil and seasonings and spread in a single layer on a baking sheet lined with parchment paper.

1. Bake the potatoes, turning occasionally, for about 30 minutes or until tender and golden brown. Dip in organic, preservative-free ketchup.

Make sure to make extra because they won't last very long!

For you were bought with a price. So glorify God in your body.

1 Corinthians 6:20

# quick and easy ratatouille: a french vegetable stew

## YOU NEED:

- 2 tablespoons grape seed or olive oil

- 1 medium onion, chopped

- 1 garlic clove, finely minced or mashed

- 1 Japanese eggplant, cut into 1/2-inch chunks (it's firmer and has fewer seeds than large eggplants)

- 1 yellow bell pepper, large pieces

- 1 medium zucchini, cut in 1/2-inch chunks

- 1 medium summer squash, cut in 1/2-inch chunks

- 1 carrot, cubed (optional)

- 1 can diced tomatoes

- 1 tablespoon capers (optional)

- 3/4 cup oil-cured black olives, pitted and sliced (optional)

- 1 teaspoon Herbes de Provence (substitute Italian seasoning and to make Capotana instead of Ratatouille)

- 1 teaspoon agave syrup (to reduce the acidity of the tomato sauce)

- salt and pepper to taste

## STEP-BY-STEP:

1. Sauté onions and garlic in a little oil for a couple of minutes over low-medium heat.

2. Add eggplant, bell pepper, zucchini, squash, and tomatoes. Season with salt and pepper and cook over medium-high heat until juice from tomatoes gets steamy and bubbly.

2. Sprinkle with herbs and mix well. Cover, and cook gently on low heat for 15 minutes, or until veggies reach desired doneness.

3. Stir in olives, capers, and a little agave syrup. Serve as a main dish with a side or brown rice.

Yields approximately 5 servings.

# vegan chili

YOU NEED:

- 1 tablespoon olive oil or grape seed oil

- 1/2 medium onion, chopped

- 2 bay leaves

- 1 teaspoon ground cumin

- 2 tablespoons dried oregano

- 2 stalks celery, chopped

- 2 green bell peppers, chopped

- 2 jalapeños, chopped (optional, very spicy!)

- 3 garlic cloves, mashed

- 2 (12 ounce) packages of meat substitute

- 3 (28 ounce) cans diced tomatoes, crushed

- 1 (15 ounce) can black beans, drained

- 1 (15 ounce) can garbanzo beans, drained (optional)

- 1 (15 ounce) can pinto beans, drained

- 1/4 cup chili powder (use more or less depending on your desired spiciness)

- 1 (15 ounce) can whole kernel corn, drained

- salt and pepper to taste

STEP-BY-STEP:

1. Heat oil in a large pot over medium heat. Sauté onions and season with salt and pepper. Add bay leaves, cumin, and oregano.

2. Cook and stir until onion is tender, then mix in the celery, green bell peppers, jalapeños, and garlic.

2. When vegetables are heated through, mix in meat substitute and brown for a couple of minutes.

3. Pour canned tomatoes and beans into the pot. Add chili powder and bring to a boil. Reduce heat to low, and simmer for 45 minutes.

4. Stir in corn, and continue cooking for 5 more minutes. Add a little vegetable stock or water if you prefer your chili a little soupier.

# gazpacho: cold tomato soup

YOU NEED:

- 1 lb. ripe tomatoes
- 1/2 red bell pepper
- 1 zucchini
- 1 garlic clove (optional)
- 1 jalapeño (optional, very spicy)
- 2 tablespoons olive oil
- 2 tablespoons lemon juice
- salt to taste

GARNISH

- 1 persian cucumber, finely diced
- 1/2 red bell pepper, finely diced
- 1/4 red onion (optional), finely diced
- olive oil to sprinkle on top

STEP-BY-STEP:

1. Pass tomatoes, pepper, zucchini, and garlic through a juice maker, according to manufacturer's directions.

2. With the motor running, add olive oil and lemon juice.

3. You may use a blender if you don't own a juicer. When blended, the texture will be slightly chunkier, but you can strain the mixture if you like a smoother consistency.

4. Season to taste and chill before serving.

5. Serve mixed garnish ingredients in a separate bowl for your guests.

Daniel Fast in the summer? Why, yes! Summertime is when you can find the best tasting and most affordable produce, like tomatoes. Heirloom varieties would add more depth and flavor if you want to get creative. It's such a vibrant and nourishing soup. It's a meal in itself.

# easy vegan pupusas

## BEAN FILLING FOR ABOUT 6 PUPUSAS:

- 1 tablespoon grape seed oil
- 1 can or about 1 1/2 cups cooked beans (pinto, black, northern or white)
- 1/4 onion, diced
- 1/2 teaspoon dried oregano leaves, crushed
- salt and pepper to taste

## QUICK CURTIDO SLAW:

- 1/2 head of cabbage, shredded (any type of cabbage)
- 1 tomato, diced
- 3 radishes, thinly sliced
- 1 jalapeño, sliced (optional)
- 1/2 teaspoon dried oregano leaves, crushed
- juice of 2 lemons
- 2 tablespoons oil
- salt and pepper to taste

## CORN DOUGH:

- 1 cup masa harina
- 1 cup warm water
- 1/4 tsp salt

Curtido is a pickled cabbage slaw. Traditionally, it is made with shredded cabbage, carrots, bell peppers, onions, oregano, and vinegar. However, here's an easy, more salad-like version that you can prepare in about 5 minutes.

Upgrade: Pupusas can be filled with any Daniel-Fast friendly ingredients. How about a mixture of sautéed soy chorizo, onions, potatoes, and zucchini? Now, that sounds like a pretty tasty upgrade!

## STEP-BY-STEP:

1. **To make the bean filling,** purée beans in a food processor or blender until smooth and set aside.

2. Heat oil in a pan over medium-low heat and sauté onions until slightly brown.

3. Add bean purée to onions and cook, stirring occasionally until it thickens, about 15-20 minutes. Season with oregano, salt, and pepper.

4. Remove from heat and cool to room temperature before stuffing pupusas.

5. The refried beans on p. 39 are great to use in pupusas, as long as beans are cooked to a thick purée. You can't stuff pupusas if beans are runny.

6. **To make the quick curtido slaw,** simply combine all vegetables in a bowl.

7. Add the lemon juice, oil, oregano, and season with salt and pepper. Mix well and serve.

8. **To make the dough,** combine masa harina with warm water and salt in a bowl.

9. Mix with your hands and knead until soft dough forms. Add more water as needed. If the dough is crumbly than you need to add more water. The dough may be too moist if it sticks to your fingers, so you may need to dust it with more flour.

10. Let dough stand for 15 minutes, covered with a wet cloth.

# Easy Pupusa Making Technique For Beginners

1. Divide dough into 5 or 6 golf sized balls and keep covered with damp cloth. This will keep the dough from drying out.

2. Place a ball of dough between two sheets of plastic wrap and press down with your hand or with a pan to flatten it like a tortilla.

3. Rub your hands with cooking oil and pull back the plastic wrap. Hold tortilla on one hand and add a generous tablespoon of beans in the center.

4. Cup the filled tortilla in your hand and squeeze to seal edges together. Moisten your hand with oil or water if the dough feels too sticky.

5. Roll into a ball and place between sheets of plastic wrap again. Flatten softly with your hands, making sure the sides don't crack.

6. Heat an oiled, non-stick skillet or pan over medium-high heat and cook pupusas for about 4 minutes on each side or until golden.

Serve pupusas with a side of curtido and a simple, smooth tomato salsa. See basic salsa recipe on p. 45.

# ACKNOWLEDGEMENTS

I have several people to thank here, but I must begin thanking Jesus for giving us the vision to create something like this. He provided the resources, wisdom, talent, and inspiration we needed. God also placed the burden in our hearts to donate some of the proceeds of this book to the orphans of Guatemala. Our hope is that by providing financial help to these children, they will have a place to be loved and sheltered, and give their lives to Jesus. Thank you all for purchasing this book and being part of such a worthy cause.

It all started with a blog and a few recipes. When our church first announced that we were going on a Daniel Fast, I immediately realized I needed some ideas and recipes. I'll be plain and honest here. At Spirit and Truth Worship Center, we love good food. In my own close-minded opinion, we have the best home cooks in Orange County! However, going vegan for almost a month was a whole new animal! That is the main reason why my husband and I started the blog, CaringCarrot.com. I really couldn't have done it without my church. Thank you for being incredible friends and leaders, and for really giving me the opportunity to share my recipes with you. I see it as a ministry that many of you encouraged me to initiate. Special thanks to Sis. Copple for believing in me and allowing me to shoot my first and only cooking show in your home. I felt truly special and for a moment, dreamt about being The Next Food Network Star. Can I say "LOL" here?

Well-deserved thanks to Art Cole, a super talented artist, for providing graphic design advise and for creating such a stunning cover for this cookbook. You and your sweet wife Lynn are amazing people and a blessing to many. Thank you Jennifer Cobb for taking time to shoot our family portrait for this book and making us look so good. You truly know how to capture life in a photo. Thank you so much for your willingness to help.

Some of the recipes in this book were partly inspired by my own youth, growing up Salvadorian in California. What does that mean? Well, it means some days we ate pupusas or fried plantains and other days we craved Chinese take-out. My culinary experiences are as diverse as the world itself so I'm thankful to God because we've had the opportunity to go on missionary trips to Asia and Europe. I love Mediterranean food as well, and to make my long story short, I tried as best as I could to represent all my foodie experiences in this cookbook.

I'd like to thank my mom for teaching me the basics of cooking when I was kid. It was extremely invaluable and my daughter Bella will inherit our rich legacy of cooking and healthy eating. We always knew we were loved because you made sure we had good food to eat. You taught us to be resourceful homemakers and cooks. To the rest of my family and friends, thanks for being such great guinea pigs and eating my Daniel Fast meals. All the words of encouragement were priceless. I love you guys.

Finally, thanks to my husband, Matt, who is actually my most valuable mentor, food tester, photographer, psychologist, and everything else in between. I could not have done it without you. As a matter of fact, you are the one who came up with the blog idea and the cookbook idea. This is our joint project. We blended our talents together in one book. Thanks for your unconditional love and support...and for doing the heaping huge piles of dishes. I'm a blessed lady.

In Jesus Name!

We are Eugenia, Matt, and Bella. I teach history for a living and I am a bit of a history geek. When Bella sleeps, I write Bible lessons for our youth group, and I also work on my cookbook ideas. Matt is a photo teacher, food photographer, blogger, Sunday school teacher, and thanks to this book, a food stylist and designer. He's a super awesome daddy and husband, too!

We live in Orange County, California. We do have a lot of orange trees here and plenty of seasonal produce that we can eat during the Daniel Fast. The weather is great. Traffic isn't. However, every week we look forward to attending a lively, Christ-loving, and caring church, Spirit and Truth Worship Center in the city of Orange.

In June 2011, we welcomed Bella-Natalia to this world. It means beautiful birth of Christ. Bella also means "God's promise" in Hebrew. She's our miracle baby. We waited and we waited. We were disappointed many times. Nonetheless, after a few Daniel Fasts plus many prayers from friends and family, we received our promise. She was born healthy and full of life. We've never had a boring day since. Life is full of surprises, disappointments, happy moments, and sad times. However, God has never failed us and he's within our reach always. What an exciting journey this is. We wouldn't trade it for anything.

I don't know how to end this, but I hope our cooking and book publishing journey doesn't end here. You can find us on CaringCarrot.com for more ideas and resources.

Photograph by Jennifer Cobb

ABOUT US
from our hearts...

ISBN-13: 978-1481024242

ISBN-10: 1481024248

Made in the USA
Lexington, KY
13 February 2015